God Will Meet You in the

Go

May God Bless

Devin D. Westbrook Sr.

God Will Meet You in the

Go

Westbrook Media & Publishing
Book Layout: Devin D. Westbrook Sr.
Cover Art: Devin D. Westbrook Sr.
Edited By: Samantha Westbrook
ISBN: 978 – 0 – 359 – 76864 - 6

I dedicate this book to every person out there who has potential. That was a word I grew sick of hearing; that is until I decided to do something about it. I pray that you would receive this as the catalysis for action. My hope is that you would reach your potential, decide to walk in it and live it out loud. This book is for you.

Table of Contents

Foreword

Creative Genius. Brilliant. Anointed. Word Play Master. My Favorite Preacher. These are all words I often use to describe the author.

I honor him for his academic accomplishments, his contributions to the community as well as his role as senior servant of Redemption Church.

I absolutely LOVE him for being the priest, prophet and provider in our home. We have been married for 12 1/2 years and we have grown together, been stretched together and we have witnessed the Power of God work in our lives together. As he evolves into this role as author it only makes sense for us to approach it and celebrate it TOGETHER.

I love him with my whole heart and I am simply grateful that God chose me to be his FAVOR. To everything that God assigns to his hands I am ready to support and I say, Ready....... Set......... Go.........

Samantha Westbrook M. Ed.

Preface

Several years ago I began toying with the idea of consulting with young pastors and church planters in regards to establishing their ministries. I felt that sharing this information was critical. From my experience, many senior pastors were either unwilling or uncertain about sharing their successes and failures. It was a truth that was unsettling for me. I had always hoped that an elder man of God would take me under his wing and pour out wisdom and instruction. I longed to be directly mentored and even rebuked when necessary. When we planted Redemption Church, we did so without any financial backing. Neither did we have the luxury of being coached by anyone who had that kind of experience. Sad to say in those early years we didn't have an encouraging voice to celebrate our wins or one to comfort our losses. I don't say this proudly but we survived those moments without a spiritual covering. I had to accept the fact that I was dealt a different set of circumstances (More on this later).

My mother once said to me, "Remember what you experienced, so that when you become a pastor you won't repeat the same mistakes." I believe that out of my humble beginnings birthed this notion to teach young pastors and church planters what I've learned. My desire is to correspondingly reverse the trend. It is important to me to help establish a kingdom where churches and pastors build and work congruently. I believe part of my assignment is to sow what I would like to see. I would like to see ministers and ministries share methodologies, strategies and resources which would better enable us to be more effective for the body of Christ.

I think you get the point about my desire to impart; however, I often considered the timing. More appropriately, to be honest, I felt as though the timing was not right. If Redemption had a building to call our own, it would validate what I had to share. That building would be proof, that I did something right, something that others could use as a model. Isn't it crazy to think that the acquisition of a piece of property is what justifies everything I've learned in the previous six years as a founding pastor?

I was conversing with a good friend of mine who had been displaced from church. In that conversation he shared with me that he didn't know how to pick back up. I said to him that he should just go. It didn't matter where he went, just go; and that God would meet him in the go. The Holy Spirit convicted me by my own words. Why am I waiting on a physical building in order to write this book? Why am I waiting on something circumstantial to take place? Just start writing; just get going and God would meet me in the go.

Chapter One

God Said Go

"When God says go forward, don't even think about standing still."

Beth Moore

Now the Lord said to Abram, "Go from your country and your kindred and your father's house to the land that I will show you. ² And I will make of you a great nation, and I will bless you and make your name great, so that you will be a blessing. ³ I will bless those who bless you, and him who dishonors you I will curse, and in you all the families of the earth shall be blessed." Genesis 12: 1-3 (ESV)

The book of Genesis lays the historical as well as theological foundation for the rest of the Bible. Since the Bible is the story of God's redemption of His people, then Genesis chapters 1-11 tells us why redemption is necessary. Understand that chapters 1-2 clearly deal with the creation of man; in chapter 3 we find the fall of man, Chapter 4 marks for us man's capacity to murder. Chapters 6-8 tell us of man's wickedness and God's judgment of man. Chapter 9 is about God's new covenant with man. Chapter 11 informs us of man's insistence for independence, which resulted in God scattering man. This brings us to chapter 12. Please understand that Chapter 12 is a pivotal chapter. It is at this point that God turns His attention from the rebelliousness of mankind to His kindness to one man in particular. This lets us know that not only is God concerned with the world in totality; He is also concerned about all of us individually. This means, to anyone who is reading this book, God is greatly concerned about you.

The psalmist David asks the question, *"What is man that you are mindful of him?"* (Psalms 8:4 ESV). What David was expressing was that creation and all of its splendor should be God's crowning achievement. Man appears to be insignificant in comparison to the grandioso of the stars and the heavens, yet God's desire is to favor man over such things. Not only does God favor man but He positions man to exercise dominion over the world and every living thing. Essentially what I am saying is that God created you for more. You are not average. You were not made to be average. Average is not in your DNA.

If God's ultimate goal was to bless Abram and to make his name great, let's look at how God accomplishes this goal. First things first, God said to him, "Go." The Cambridge Dictionary suggests that the word go means to move, to proceed, to advance, progress or travel to another place or in a particular direction. Furthermore, it means to become or be in a certain condition. Therefore, the unfolding of Abram's future was founded in God's command to go. Successes that awaited him were secured in God's command to go. A future nation and even the redemption of the world rested in God's command to go. The promise of future blessings were or should I say are packed in God's command to go.

My nephew Zavian has become quite the track and field competitor. As a younger child no

> *The promise of future blessings are packed in God's command to go.*

one recognized in him any characteristics of an extraordinary athlete. He didn't seem to jump really high. He didn't display an exceptional ability to move swiftly, quite the contrary to say the least. However, he shocked everyone when he began to experience success in this sport. Yet, he never crosses a finish line, he never receives a medal unless he responds swiftly to the command of go. God said go. I wonder how many of us are settling for average? I wonder how many of us are forfeiting our future because of our failure to obey? How many of us are leaving money on the table? How many of us are not walking in the will of God for our lives? How many of us are stuck in dead end jobs? How many of us just exist in relationships that have long since expired? How many of us are living below our capacity because of our failure to comply with God's command to go? It was Best Selling author and motivational speaker Les Brown who said and I quote, "The graveyard is the richest place on earth, because it is here that you will find all the hopes and dreams that were never fulfilled, the books that were never written, the songs that were never sang, the inventions that were never shared, the cures that were never discovered, all because someone was too afraid to take that first step." When God said go, I wonder how many of us stood still?

Then David asked the LORD, "Should I chase after this band of raiders? Will I catch them?" And the LORD told him, "Yes, go after them. You will surely recover everything that was taken from you!" 1 Samuel 30:8 (NLT)

God assured David that if he pursued his enemies that victory would be his. Notice in the text there is a principle of causation. David's ability to recover everything was the residual effect of God's command to go. He had God's word that it would work out in his favor. God said go and by going he knew that he was going to win. Just like David we have God's word. If you've attended church for any length of time

I'm sure you heard it said, "If God says it, that settles it." God has spoken. And when God speaks we understand that His word is the authority. You have God's word.

Let me quickly refute what many of you may be thinking? I'm sure somebody who is reading this is convinced that you are not in the best position to do much about your current situation. Someone reading this is convinced that you're either too old, not financially situated, not sure if you're physically able or maybe the timing is just not right. Consider the prophet Ezekiel if you will. Ezekiel helps us to realize that even in the low places life can spring forward. God told him to prophesy to the dry bones in the valley. As he prophesied in that valley, what was dead began to live again.

The hand of the Lord was upon me, and he brought me out in the Spirit of the Lord and set me down in the middle of the valley; it was full of bones. ² And he led me around among them, and behold, there were very many on the surface of the valley, and behold, they were very dry. ³ And he said to me, "Son of man, can these bones live?" And I answered, "O Lord God, you know." ⁴ Then he said to me, "Prophesy over these bones, and say to them, O dry bones, hear the word of the Lord. ⁵ Thus says the Lord God to these bones: Behold, I will cause breath to enter you, and you shall live. ⁶ And I will lay sinews upon you, and will cause flesh to come upon you, and cover you with skin, and put breath in you, and you shall live, and you shall know that I am the Lord." ⁷ So I prophesied as I was commanded. And as I prophesied, there was a sound, Ezekiel 37: 1-7 (ESV)

Man of God, woman of God you have a multitude of distractions and discouragement but never minimize the power to decree a thing. You have the authority to speak and to declare. You don't have to settle for your situation, speak life over yourself. Take command over your life. No excuses. Now, let's go!

Notes

_____

_____

_____

_____

_____

_____

_____

_____

_____

Chapter Two

We Are Called to Go

"But beware of this about callings: they may not lead us where we intended to go or even where we want to go. If we choose to follow, we may have to be willing to let go of the life we already planned and accept whatever is waiting for us. And if the calling is true, though we may not have gone where we intended, we will surely end up where we need to be."

Steve Goodier

Now the Lord said to Abram, "Go from your country and your kindred and your father's house to the land that I will show you. ²And I will make of you a great nation, and I will bless you and make your name great, so that you will be a blessing. ³I will bless those who bless you, and him who dishonors you I will curse, and in you all the families of the earth shall be blessed." Genesis 12: 1-3 (ESV)

I grew up in a time when children would actually go outside to play. We understood the rule of going outside. It was, if you do not have permission, don't go too far. In all likelihood someone was going to call your name and you better be close enough to hear it. I often remember my grandmother calling us back into the house so that we could walk to the grocery store for her. Of course this was a time before cell phones. Grandmother wasn't texting; she was literally going to call us. She would stand on the front porch, yell our names with the expectation that we would hear her and come running. That was a simpler time. Parents didn't worry about allowing their children to walk to the corner store. Back then was a time in which everybody in the neighborhood knew who we were and who we were connected to. There was a greater sense of accountability and responsibility. One of the primary expectation of children in that day was to be obedient. If an elder called, you responded and you did so in a timely manner.

Let us understand that God's word for Abram to "Go" is considered to be a command. He had given Abram a directive or an order. Yet allow me to make this clear distinction here. There is a difference between God's command and our calling. The two are closely related, however, the two differ in terms of ownership. Abram heard God's command and yet made the decision to comply. In other words, he answered the call to go.

I will never forget when I became certain that there was a call of God on my life! I was attending a revival at my

15

home church, business as usual I suppose. I grew up in church, so being at church was nothing short of ordinary. I often say I grew up on the choir side of the church, so the ministry or preaching side typically did not capture my attention. Don't get me wrong, I understood what I understood but as far as revelation and illumination goes... Don't judge me. At least I was in the house. Okay, let's focus. I was in revival when I began to sense that the woman of God who was ministering that night was speaking directly to me. This was different. Sure I'd heard preaching before but never had I felt as though the message was directly speaking to me. In some way I began to feel as though I was inserted into the moment. So I began to inquire of God. "Lord are you calling me to preach," I asked? I got very specific with God that night. I asked Him to confirm in this certain particular way so that I would know that this was His will concerning my life. No sooner than I made my request known God answered in just that way.

What I know now that I did not know then was more so than a calling to preach, God was calling me to go from religion to relationship. There is a difference. Religion is a personal set or an institutionalized system of attitudes, beliefs and practices. A person could watch basketball religiously. A relationship on the other hand is different. A relationship is the state of being connected. It's a kinship. God was calling me from a practice into an opportunity to come to know Him more personally.

I'm trying to convey that God's command for us to go is also our calling to go from. *"Now the Lord said to Abram, Go from your country and your kindred and your father's house."* So essentially God's command to Abram was for him to go from his country, go from his comforts and go from his customs. I believe many of us can realistically relate to this command. Like Abram, I was comfortable in my ways. I went to church religiously. I sang in the choir religiously. When in Rome do as the Romans do, therefore, in church I did what church folk do, religiously. But that night at revival God spoke to me to go from religion to relationship.

Let me suggest to you that God has a way of crashing in on your comfort zone. He has a way of interrupting your itinerary. You might find comfort in the

> *God has a way of crashing in on your comfort zone.*

comfort zone but God is calling you to come out of that place. *"Now the Lord said to Abram, Go from your country and your kindred and your father's house."* Listen, some of us have become too comfortable in the lifestyle in which we live. Some of us have become too comfortable where we work, as well as the position that we've grown accustomed to operating in. Some of us are way too comfortable interfacing with folk who are not favorable for our future. Just because there is a history does not give validity to continued interactions. Some of us have grown too comfortable going to the wrong places and doing the wrong things. We must be careful about being too comfortable. Old folks used to say, "You can't teach an old dog new tricks." What they were trying to tell us is that the older we get the more difficult it is to adapt to anything different. In other words, don't get stuck in your comfort zone. Don't get stuck in your mess.

In an attempt to be real rounded let me suggest to you, not only can you get stuck in your mess but you can also get stuck in your success.

17 As He was setting out on a journey, a man ran up to Him and knelt before Him, and asked Him, "Good Teacher, what shall I do to inherit eternal life?" 18 And Jesus said to him, "Why do you call Me good? No one is good except God alone. 19 You know the commandments, 'Do not murder, Do not commit adultery, Do not steal, Do not bear false witness, Do not defraud, Honor your father and mother.'" 20 And he said to Him, "Teacher, I have kept all these things from my youth up." 21 Looking at him, Jesus felt a love for him and said to

19

him, *"One thing you lack: go and sell all you possess and give to the poor, and you will have treasure in heaven; and come, follow Me."* [22] *But at these words he was saddened, and he went away grieving, for he was one who owned much property. Mark 10: 17-22 (NASB)*

Isn't it great to enjoy some successes in life? We've been told all of our lives that if we work hard enough we could become successful. There is nothing wrong with having a good career, making good money, having a family and a few nice things. We should take full advantage of educational opportunities. We should be proud to attain degrees and other certifications. However, I believe that the young man in the Markan narrative is an illustration to us that we should be cautious not to place more value on our resources than in the Source. Even in the successes of life God may be requiring of you to go from your country, go from your comforts and even go from your customs.

Notes

_____

_____

_____

_____

_____

_____

_____

_____

_____

Chapter Three

Get Prepared to Go

"It's better to be prepared than to get ready."

Will Smith

August 6, 2006, a day I shall never forget. It was Sunday morning, matter of a fact it was my mother's birthday; I woke up to the chatter of next-door neighbors. When I glanced out of my bedroom window I discovered that it wasn't just my neighbor but the entire street was out and accompanied by local law enforcement officers. Sensing the severity of the moment, I decided to join the gathering. When I stepped outside, an officer briefed me on the details of their visit. As it were, the night before a group of young people had the bright idea that they would egg every vehicle parked on our block. Coincidentally, my truck that was parked in the front of our home was not touched; however, the officer recommended that I file a report just as my neighbors had done. As a show of solidarity I agreed to the request. Little did I know that this decision would be a life altering decision.

I went back into the house to get my license and inform Samantha my (then) fiancé' of the matter. Afterwards I located my wallet and returned to the officer to finish the report. Everything went as routine as expected, nothing about the moment was heightened or appeared irregular.

As we all prepared to disperse and return into our homes, the officer asked to share a brief word with me in private. As politely and discreetly as possible he accompanied me into my home. Confused and curious I looked at him awaiting a word to part from his lips. Can you imagine the level of anxiety and anticipation that was building in me simultaneously? I'd never seen a Caucasian policeman standing in an African American home seem so timid and uncomfortable, almost appearing nervous. This made me even the more nervous. Slowly he began to inform me that there had been a warrant issued for my arrest. Right then and there I lost consciousness and passed out. Okay, I didn't really pass out but in retrospect I can't see how I didn't. I mean that was as unexpected as it gets. It does something to me now as I write this.

Let's get back to the story. Now please consider that I had never had any kind of contact with police in my life. To that point I had never been to jail nor had I experienced any kind of legal issues. To that end, imagine if you will the jolt that went through me when he broke the news. It seemed as though time stood still. I struggled to process what was taking place. I'd never thought of myself as a criminal. I mean sure I'd ran a couple of stop signs and amassed some speeding tickets and a few even went unpaid, but a criminal I was not. Yet I was about to suffer the humility and the shame that every criminal suffered. To make matters worse it happened in my living room and in front of my girl. I'm not sure if I felt more saddened and disappointed for her or for myself. I felt helpless to say the least. Additionally, I had to grasp the reality, that freedom, as I've always known it was about to be snatched away. Unbeknown to anyone I was a deserter and had gone AWOL from the United States Army. After about five years or so I had grown too comfortable in that condition. It was time for me to go.

If someone would've told me that I would spend the next nine days of my life in a jail cell, under the harsh confines of the twenty-three and one lockdown, I would've cursed them to their face. Twenty-three and one means to be locked in a jail cell for twenty-three hours of the day with only one hour outside of the cell. Usually this is reserved for those who have committed serious crimes; violent offenses like murders and such. It's highly unusual for someone whose circumstances were like mine to be treated in that manner. I consider myself to be a rather tough guy. I don't back down nor do I scare easily. I'd be misleading you if I communicated that I wasn't afraid. I was. In fact, out of the two hundred and sixteen plus hours I spent in that place, for about five consecutive hours, I was scared to death. The walk down that long dark corridor of cellblock D, being yelled at and challenged by people I perceived to be lowest of the low, was by far the most intimidating moment I'd ever experienced. In my mind they were like ravaging pit bulls being forcefully retained as fresh meat was being dangled in their presence. That was my Green Mile moment. Then to make it to my cell and find that there was someone, a total stranger for that matter, on the inside that I would be locked away with was horrifying. Finally to hear the cell slam shut knowing that no amount of effort could reverse what was taking place was terrifying. My mind began to conjure up fears that I'd never thought possible. The unknown is a horrible place. I didn't know where I was, with whom I was there with and how long I would be there with them. I was not prepared for the possibility and potentiality of such a place. For a span of about five consecutive hours I lived in that fear.

25 About midnight Paul and Silas were praying and singing hymns to God, and the prisoners were listening to them, 26 and suddenly there was a great earthquake, so that the foundations of the prison were shaken. And immediately all the doors were opened, and everyone's bonds were unfastened. Acts 16: 25-26 (ESV)

The biblical account of Paul and Silas is by far one of my favorite passages. It's amazing to me how two men whose lives were hanging in the balance could have that kind of confidence in God. It's a wonderful testament of how praise and worship in such a problematic situation has the potential to produce such power and a strong move of God. As a minister, when I feel the need to shift the room this passage has become my go to.

Allow me to demonstrate- Let's have church! The Bible says that about midnight Paul and Silas were praying and singing hymns to God and the other prisoners were listening to them. Suddenly there was such a violent earthquake that the foundations of the prison were shaken. At once all the prison doors flew open, and everyone's chains came loose. In other words, when the anointed of God comes into agreement God will shift the atmosphere. Grab your neighbor by the hand. Rock them and shake them. Shake them and rock them. I feel a move of God in this place. Chains are falling in this place. Deliverance has shown up in this place. There's a breakthrough that's about to breakout in this place. Somebody shout in this room!!!

I'd love to tell you that I had that kind of confidence in God when I found myself in that situation, but I did not. However, something strange did happen that night. No, the foundations of the jail did not shake. No, the doors of our cells did not swing open however my proverbial chains did fall off. About midnight, I began to hear prisoners cry out to

God. To be clear, I am not paraphrasing the text. Literally about midnight those men who were in their cells, whom I previously perceived to be ravages and the lowest of the low, began calling on the name of the Lord. I would bet that I was probably the most religious person on my cellblock, but I was not the first partaker of this radical praise. I wasn't even praying for myself. When I heard the praise of those people I felt a peace come over me. It was in that moment that I heard God speak into my spirit, "I'll handle your problem, if you would only get in My presence." I began to sense that God was not punishing me. He was preparing me.

I believe the same is true for you. What you perceived to be problematic God was using to prepare you for the promise. Just as the olive is crushed to produce the oil, God will use your pain and your past to prepare you. Being broke prepared you to be a better manager of money. Being mishandled prepared you to better handle things that God handed to you. Failed relationships should only prepare you to become better in the next one.

> *God was not punishing me. He was preparing me.*

In 1955, Noah McVicker of Cincinnati was commissioned to develop a product that would clean coal from wallpaper. Shortly after creating it, the market for the cleaning putty began to diminish drastically. Desperate and on the verge of bankruptcy, he soon discovered that children enjoyed playing with the product. So he began to manufacture and market the putty as a child's toy and named it Play-Doh. By 1958, Play-Doh's sales reached nearly 3 million dollars.

God will use your pressure and your pain in order to prepare you to go to the next level. What did not kill you only served to make you more prepared. What the devil meant for evil, God was using as a tool. He's been Miyagi

31

(ing) you (Karate Kid circa 1984). You didn't know it but what you went through was only training you to fight.

Notes

_____

_____

_____

_____

_____

_____

_____

_____

_____

Chapter Four

Everybody Can't Go

"You're going to lose people along the way, but remember not everyone is intended to go with you."

Tony Gaskin

Now the Lord said to Abram, "Go from your country and your kindred and your father's house to the land that I will show you. Genesis 12:1 (ESV)

In retrospect I now distinguish 2006 as a painful yet purposeful transitional year in my life. Professionally, I went from being a highly favorable candidate for a manager's position on my job to completely losing my job. Personally, friendships that date back to adolescence were not only diminished but drastically damaged. The rapport amongst my peers was nowhere near what it once was. The group I had grown accustomed to doing life with no longer felt like my group. The whispers that I received from a few down low loyalist (friends who quietly and secretly attempted to remain friends) confirmed what I believed. I had become the guy on the outside. Just a few months prior I was certainly an inside guy. I say this to paint a picture not as an opportunity to boast, but I was fine Devin (I didn't make up that name, trust me). Upon walking into the room I commanded attention. At least that's what my ego led me to believe. Now I was no longer welcome in the room. What was most confusing was that my only intention was to better myself. I wasn't interested in changing my circle. I was not interested in calling them to the carpet because of what I could not longer do. In all honesty, I still enjoyed their frivolous lifestyles. Through them I was still vicariously living that life. I mean I knew God was working in me but I wasn't at all there yet, far from it.

What was going on with me was really just about me. I only desired something different for myself. However, I quickly realized that it wasn't just that people didn't like change, I discovered that they resented it. As a result, I became the focus of that resentment. I admit I was hurt and stunned at just how quickly things had changed. It's been said that time usually brings about a change. But the change that I experienced had nothing to do with time, it had everything to do with the decision that I made to go.

Notice the text says, *"Now the Lord said to Abram, "Go from your country and your kindred and your father's house to the land that I will show you."* It's apparent to me now that God's command to

> *God's command to go requires sacrifice.*

go required sacrifice. Abram was fully expected to leave his family behind. Any and everything that had been familiar, God was calling for him to go from.

Abram was believed to be at the ripe old age of about seventy-five years old. This is not the oldest of old biblically speaking, but it's still well past his prime years. His father is deceased and by assuming responsibility for Lot, his nephew, we can deduce that the mantle of leadership in his family fell on his shoulders. In the ancient Mesopotamian culture the practice of Patriarchal Paganistic Religion was a tradition. Abram would've ascribed to polytheism (many gods) and not monotheism (one god). There was a belief that a relationship would be fostered with a particular family god, which undertook the divine sponsorship of that family. "Therefore family worship was directed to this god with the expectation that protection and guidance would be provided." (Cultural Background Study Bible, Zondervan: 2019). Not to mention there was a geographical limitation associated with family gods. Can I suggest to you that leaving from his country, from his family and from his culture, Abram was breaking deeply rooted religious ties? This is equivalent to a Christian child who had been raised in the faith departing from that faith in favor of an unknown religion.

According to the text, Abram was commanded to leave. However, leaving meant to abandon any and everything that formulated his perception of living. Leaving meant to leave his family and those connected to him hanging in the balance. Leaving meant departing from childhood friends and the social gatherings that he'd come to love. Leaving meant that there would be no more hanging out at the well during the cool of the day. Leaving meant walking away from life as he'd known it to be. God's command to go required sacrifice. *"Now the Lord said to Abram, Go from your country and your kindred and your father's house to the land that I will show you."* In other words, Abram everybody can't go.

Let's give Abram credit for such a faith filled act to follow a God whom he did not know. However, let us also learn from his disobedience. Yes, Abram did go from his country. Yes, Abram did go from his father's house. But notice that Abram does not completely leave his kindred. *"So Abram went, as the Lord had told him, and Lot went with him." (Genesis 12:4 ESV).* Look at the result of his disobedience. Because Lot went with him, Lot and Abram suffered a strain in their relationship, which caused them to separate from each other. Because Lot went with him, Abram was forced to war against the Kings who took Lot into captivity. Because Lot went with him, Abram found himself reasoning with God not to destroy Sodom. Because Lot went with him, Lot's wife would be turned into a pillar of salt and his daughters would become instigators of an incestuous relationship that birthed wicked kinsmen. What would've happened to Lot had he stayed, I don't know. What I do know is that the text illustrates to us the residual impact of allowing people to partake of a journey that God has not called them to participate in. In other words everybody can't go.

I wonder how many of us are suffering because we're trying to hold on to a relationship that God has called us to go from? How many of us are wandering through life purposelessly because our loyalties yet remain to what God has called us to go from? How many of us are wasting years holding on to the pain that someone inflicted upon us? They don't deserve that space in our lives; God has called us to go from. I don't know to whom this is for but I feel led to let you know that there are some people that's been clinging on to you that in this season of your life you're going to have to release and let go. It's something about their hold on you that's essentially holding you back from your next level. The Bible calls them parasitic; these parasitic people are pulling on you and preventing you from purpose. It was the O'Jays who sang, "I guess You've Got your hooks in me." I've come to discover that some of us have leeches in our lives that we've allowed to latch on to us for far too long. I dare you to shout right now, "Loose me and let me go."

Ladies, that brother that's good in bed but he keeps messing up your head. It's time to let him go. That sister that looks good from behind but she's really messing up your mind. It's time to let her go. That BFF that you think is a best friend forever but the truth of the matter is that they're your best friend failure, baby it's time to let them go. I declare freedom from mama's mess and daddy's demons. You're free from that person who violated you. You're free from that person who has been tormenting you. You're free from other people's expectation of you. It is time for you to go and the harsh reality is everybody can't go.

When Jesus went into the bedroom of the young girl who was dead, the bible says that He put everybody on the outside of the room, took the girl by the hand and raised her up (Matthew 9: 25). On the night that Jesus was betrayed, He took the disciples to the Garden of Gethsemane. He made everyone remain outside of the garden with the exception of Peter, James and John whom He took into the garden with Him. God's command to go carries with it an expectation to go to as well as an expectation to go from. There are times in life when what God is calling you to require sacrifice. There are seasons in which everybody you know and love simply cannot go with you. Everybody can't go.

I've learned that many of us are loyal to people who are not loyal to us. They fail to support your convictions yet they would rather feed your addictions. In my experience, those persons usually reveal themselves. Don't be afraid to walk away. Your life may depend on it. I pray that God will give you discernment to decipher who is good for your life in this season.

Notes

<u>Chapter Five</u>

God Will Meet You In The Go

"The Lord replied: "My precious child, I love you and would never leave you. During your times of trials and suffering, when you see only one set of footprints, it was then that I carried you."

Mary Stevenson

After my little mini vacation, or more accurately an involuntary nine-day stay away, I was released and given orders to report to Fort Hood, Texas. I was not detained until pick up as suggested. I was not transported there with chains on my hands and my feet. I was all but certain that a U.S. Marshall was in route to transport me and hand deliver me over to the Army. Oddly enough, I was given a ticket to report there on my own recognizance, something no one expected would happen.

As I prepared to report fear began to creep back into my thoughts. The speculation of what would happen to me when I arrived had begun to take on a life of its own. Would I be court-martialed? If so, how much time would I have to serve? On average, time served for a case of desertion was undoubtedly confinement of up to three to five years. Even if pleading my case went favorably, the amount of time served was still 18 months to two years of confinement. So quite naturally, as I drew nearer to my report date fear of the unknown began to war against my mind. It's something that I discovered in that moment, something that I often share with our church; what I found out was that faith and feelings are not compatible. Everything in me said do not go. Why would you willingly surrender yourself to the worst-case scenario? To not report seriously presented itself as a plausible solution. But I had to make a decision. Would I prefer to remain in a state of fear and constantly looking over my shoulder? Perhaps it would be best if I got on the bus to face the unforeseen future. After all I created this situation. Would it even be fair to force my family to live with that kind of burden due to my own cowardice?

Therefore, I decided to leave everything behind, get on that bus and go.

I don't doubt for a moment that Abram must have had a myriad of thoughts and emotions that were swirling through his mind. Like me, I'm sure that he received a great deal of well intentioned advise from friends and family. At the end of the day he had to make a decision. Maybe he even counted the cost. Yes, God did present to him an overwhelming proposition. Look at the text. Notice verses 2-3 to be exact:

"Go from your country and your kindred and your father's house to the land that I will show you. 2 And I will make of you a great nation, and I will bless you and make your name great, so that you will be a blessing. 3 I will bless those who bless you, and him who dishonors you I will curse, and in you all the families of the earth shall be blessed. 4 So Abram went." Genesis 12:1-4 (ESV)

We know that he was called to go from, which is an undoubtedly a difficult task. Yet notice where he was called

48

to go to, *"The land that I will show you."* There isn't anything definitive about the destination that he would be directed to. Perhaps that land could've been a wasteland. It could've been dangerous and even undesirable. There is no way that he could know for sure. Abram just had to trust the word of a God that he'd never worshipped. Don't read so fast that you miss what I just said. Abram had to trust a God that he had never previously worshipped. This was a God that he did not have a prior relationship with. Yet this unknown, unseen God arrests his attention with this proposition to go. Excuse my urban vernacular for a moment but, "Where they do that at?"

Lest you miss the rest of the text, God also says to him, in essence, if you would yield to My command to go, I will then bless you and make your name great. And the text says, "So Abram went."

There is a principle that I believe is made possible through this passage. I am a firm believer that God will meet you in the go. This is a faith move. When you decide to comply to the call to go you will not have everything that you will need. You will not have all of the directions and instructions that you'll need. As a matter of fact, much of what you need will not be given until you go. That's why it requires faith. Faith functions best when you don't know and you don't have. Can I suggest to you that God will meet you in the go! I've come to discover that placed within God's petition is the promise of His presence. His promise to Abram is that if he would go from, that God Himself would show him where to go to. That's the promise of His presence. In other words, God will meet you in the go. Maybe you need further proof.

> *Placed within God's petition is the promise of His presence.*

- *Even though I walk through the valley of the shadow of death, I will fear no evil, for you are with me." Psalms (23:4 ESV)*

- *24 Then King Nebuchadnezzar was astonished and rose up in haste. He declared to his counselors, "Did we not cast three men bound into the fire?" They answered and said to the king, "True, O king." 25 He answered and said, "But I see four men unbound, walking in the midst of the fire, and they are not hurt; and the appearance of the fourth is like a son of the gods. Daniel 3: 24-25 (ESV)*

- *When evening came, he was there alone, 24 but the boat by this time was a long way from the land, beaten by the waves, for the wind was against them. 25 And in the fourth watch of the night he came to them, walking on the sea. Matthew 14: 23-25 (ESV)*

- *13 That very day two of them were going to a village named Emmaus, about seven miles from Jerusalem, 14 and they were talking with each other about all these things that had happened. 15 While they were talking and discussing together, Jesus himself drew near and went with them. Luke 24: 13-15 (ESV)*

Information is good but you don't need all of the information, just go. You don't have to know how it's going to work out. It's not your job to know, it's your job to go. It will never work out anyway if you don't go. People of faith should never allow fear to cause paralysis; we're called to go. Don't wait until it looks like the right time to go, just go. You don't need anybody's amen nor do you need their affirmation, just go. Start that business. Launch that ministry. Move to that new location. Enroll in that school. Go get that degree. Submit that application. Apply for that loan. Write that book. God promises His presence even in that place. Abram was called to go, he went and God met him in the go.

Notes

_____

_____

_____

_____

_____

_____

_____

_____

_____

Chapter Six

Provisions in the Go

"God is always doing 10,000 things in your life, you may be aware of three of them."

John Piper

3 I will bless those who bless you, and him who dishonors you I will curse, and in you all the families of the earth shall be blessed." Genesis 12: 3 (ESV)

I recall being so nervous as the bus drew nearer to the terminal in Austin, Texas. As soon as the bus parked Samantha and I immediately noticed positioned near the door of the terminal stood two policemen. I thought to myself, "Well this is it. Let's get this thing over with." I was all but ready to walk up to them and release myself into their custody. As I thought to move, I felt a prompting to be still. Then it dawned on me that they had no intention of arresting anyone. They were just causally manning their posts.

As the other passengers made their way off, Samantha looked at me and breathed a sigh of relief. Bless her heart. She was just as nervous as I was. Since it has been so many years ago, I can properly reflect on this now. I can only imagine the pressure she felt, having to wait and wonder when the worst would happen. However, it meant everything to me for her to be there. This was certainly one of the most fearful and difficult moments of my life and she wanted nothing more than to share in those moments with me. For her to be there alongside of me, holding my hand, was more comforting than she could ever imagine. When God told Abram to go, Sarai went too. When I went, Samantha went too.

We remained seated and continued on to the next stop, Killeen, Texas still yet unaware of what to expect upon arrival. As scheduled, we made it to our destination. Again to our surprise no one seemed at all apprehensive about my arrival. There wasn't anyone on high alert, there were no guards waiting to escort me to any kind of confinement. As a matter of a fact, when we made it there it was the middle of the night. No one was there expecting me at all. I can't at all express the level of confusion that I had. I mean I had all these thoughts living in my mind about what to expect. I was trying to prep myself for what I thought was the inevitable. I truly anticipated something much worse than what we were actually experiencing. The words frantic and paranoid would accurately describe what I was feeling. Yet the night was still and calm to say the least. Therefore, we caught a cab and checked into a nearby hotel to get a peaceful night of sleep.

Not only does God promise us His presence in the go, but we also have the blessed assurance of His provisions. He professes to Abram that He would bless those who were a blessing to him. For those who thought it pleasing to curse him, well God would indeed reciprocate. In the latter verses of chapter twelve, Abram and

> *Not only does God promise His presence in the go, but we also have the blessed assurance of His provision.*

Sarai, his wife journeyed into Egypt. In fear of his life because of Sarai's beauty, he instructs her to announce him as her brother; that his life might be spared. Just as he feared, the Egyptians recognized how beautiful she was and thought to kill Abram that they might take her as their own. For her sake, Abram's life was spared. However, for the Egyptians it was too late. Had they known that God said, "I will curse those who curse you" maybe than Pharaoh would've made a different decision. The Bible says,

"17 But the Lord afflicted Pharaoh and his house with great plagues because of Sarai, Abram's wife. 18 So Pharaoh called Abram and said, "What is this you have done to me? Why did you not tell me that she was your wife? 19 Why did you say, 'She is my sister,' so that I took her for my wife? Now then, here is your wife; take her, and go." 20 And Pharaoh gave men orders concerning him, and they sent him away with his wife and all that he had. Genesis 12: 17-20 (ESV)

Allow me to share with you what I call the Gospel of Fast Food. What is the Gospel of Fast Food? The genius of the fast food industry is that they claim to meet the needs of millions worldwide. According to Matt Sena, who wrote in his article *"Fast Food Industry Analysis 2018"* he says, "Globally, fast food generates revenue of over $570 billion – that is bigger than the economic value of most countries." The success of the fast food industry is that it provides a sense of convenience. Many of us live increasingly busy lives and fast food restaurants allow us the opportunity to get inexpensive meals on the go. Parents whose work schedules are more demanding can still provide food for their families because they are afforded an opportunity to get meals on the go. It's convenient in that even if the stop was unplanned, as most of us with children have discovered, you were able to meet the need on the go. For those of us, like myself, who fail to eat breakfast before leaving home, there are restaurants conveniently position to provide a meal on the go.

I'd like to believe that God performs in the same manner. He meets us in the go. God does not always permit us to know how He's going to work things out. As people of

God, as kingdom citizens, we are called to walk by faith and not according to what we can see. He expects us by faith to just go and believe that all of our needs will be met. God will meet us in the go. It is not always convenient but He is consistent. The unknown author of Hebrews declares that God, "Rewards those who seek Him." (Hebrews 11: 6 ESV). Reward, meaning to gift or to give something.

Not only do we have the promise of His presence, we also have the promise of provision. Provision is defined as the action of providing or supplying something for use. I have discovered along my journey that many times in life we don't always know what we need until we really need it. This should fuel our gratitude towards God because we have the assurance that He shall supply all our needs. The reality is that many times God in His sovereignty elects to meet us at the very point of our needs. The songwriter tells us that He may not come when you want Him to come but He's always right on time. He's consistent. In other words, there are

provisions in the go. It's in the go that He makes miracles

happen. It's in the go that He'll meet you at the point of your

needs. It's in the go that He releases His outstretched hands.

- *When he saw them he said to them, "Go and show yourselves to the priests." And as they went they were cleansed. Luke 17: 14 (ESV)*

- *21 Moses held out his hand over the sea, and the Lord drove the sea back with a strong east wind. It blew all night and turned the sea into dry land. The water was divided, 22 and the Israelites went through the sea on dry ground, with walls of water on both sides. Exodus 14: 21-22 (GNT)*

- *12 As he drew near to the gate of the town, behold, a man who had died was being carried out, the only son of his mother, and she was a widow, and a considerable crowd from the town was with her. 13 And when the Lord saw her, he had compassion on her and said to her, "Do not weep." 14 Then he came up and touched the bier, and the bearers stood still. And he said, "Young man, I say to you, arise." Luke 7: 12-14 (ESV)*

- *27 And as Jesus passed on from there, two blind men followed him, crying aloud, "Have mercy on us, Son of David." 28 When he entered the house, the blind men came to him, and Jesus said to them, "Do you believe that I am able to do this?" They said to him, "Yes,*

Lord." ²⁹ Then he touched their eyes, saying, "According to your faith be it done to you." ³⁰ And their eyes were opened. Matthew 9: 27-30 (ESV)

I enclosed these particular scriptures with the hope that they will strengthen your resolve to go. Maybe I should hope that your faith would be strengthened. It is not our job to know, it is our job to go. Can I suggest to you that faith functions best when we don't know? It is our faith that pleases God. Not only does our faith please God but also our faith prompts God to perform. Some things you will never gain access to unless you move. It is only when you go through a storm that you come to see God as shelter. It is only when you go through trials in your body that you come to see God as healer. It is when you're in need that you accurately know Him as Jehovah Jireh, the Lord who provides.

Notes

Chapter Seven

It's Still A Go

Man says, "Show me and I'll trust you," God says, "Trust Me and I'll show you."

Unknown

It's still a go. What do I mean by that statement? The definitive word here is still. I don't mean still in the sense of being still or a state of paralysis, I mean still in a progressive manner. The word still in this context functions as an indicator of continuance. For example, I'm still here. It's still a go suggests that if God were to call me to go right now my answer is still yes.

Let's reason for a moment. It is not beyond my realm of comprehension to believe that a whole yes would be the general consensus for everyone in whom God reveals Himself to. The reality is that based upon our experiences many of us find it difficult to trust. All of us have survived some kind of traumatic experience such as abuse, death, betrayal, an illness, etc. Therefore, when it appears to be an opportunity to trust God it looks more like a trigger. It triggers a moment that many of us would prefer not to relive. Here's a question, how do we trust God when we have developed trust issues? I get it, based upon the issues of our past it becomes difficult to fully trust in the present. I could say that unlike man, God is 100% dependable and trustworthy. I could say that the teachings of the Bible are clear in that God can be trusted in a way that human beings cannot be. I could say that we should not allow the faults and failures of humanity to rob us of the comfort of God's dependability. I

> *How do we trust God when we have trust issues?*

believe that trusting in God is a byproduct of trying God. If the Bible is right when it says that we overcome by the blood of the Lamb and by our testimony (Rev. 12:11), then allow me to continue sharing my testimony in hopes that it will cause you to try God to the point of trusting God.

God Will Meet You In The Go

As I prepared to be presented to the company commander in regards to the nature of my presence, I pondered if this was the anticipated point of me being apprehended. I found myself standing in front of a man that I did not know. The only thing he knew of me was not at all favorable. What he knew was that I was a deserter, some random guy who had gone AWOL and got caught. At first glance, I discerned that he was a stern and strict professional. His uniform was pressed to perfection. The awards in his office were innumerable. The scowl on his face was one born of rigorous combat exposure. He was a hardened man and my hopes was that his heart wasn't as hardened as he appeared to be.

I stood in front of this man for what seemed to be an eternity and his silence was as loud as any voice I'd ever heard. His eyes were burning a hole in my chest. Then he spoke. His harsh critiques and vile vernacular were such that it could make casual vulgarities seem like church language. After about ten minutes of what I considered a verbal assault and threats of confinement, he proceeded to let up. Unexpectedly the way I walked into his office, I walked out of his office; free. I was given a uniform, placed on active duty without a daily assignment, received regular duty pay, a barracks room to call my own; with the luxury to drive back and forth to Memphis when I desired to make weekend visits. Yes, the threat of serving time was a real possibility but the weight of it was being lifted daily.

For the next seven months of my life God would hide me in what I believe was my own personal seminary experience. I read scripture to the likes in which I had never read before. For the first time in my life I had an anointing that would drive me to read the Bible from cover to cover. Day in and day out I studied and prayed. God led me to sermons that were divinely inspired to speak to where I was in my life and to push me to where He was leading me. How could I ever forget the inspiring and faith building lessons that I received from the literature of Joel Osteen, Myles Monroe and Billy Graham just to name a few. Daily I was in the very presence of God. It was during this time that God not only confirmed my calling to the preaching ministry but He allowed me to even marry my best friend, the beautiful Samantha Westbrook. The favor of God was on my life in such an amazing way. Even though the Army Advocate attorneys sought to court martial me, God would use the same company commander to set me free. The same man whose office I stood in just seven months prior; the same man who called me every name under the sun; the same man who threatened to lock me up and throw away the key. God used that same man to not only recommend it but also sign off on a document that would send me home with my freedom. I was later told by one of the soldiers that there was a running wager on how much time the Army would give me. What they didn't bank on was that God had other plans for my life.

Had I listened to all of that well intentioned advise from family and friends, it could've gone a different way. For the first time in my life I relented of my way and decided to try God. It was in that season of my life that God took me from religion to relationship. It was in that season of my life that He provided for me at every turn. It was in that season of my life that He protected me and pulled me out of the figurative prison that I was in. Not only did God tell me to go but also He kept His promise to be present with me and provide for me. Just as He did when He provided for Abram.

"Go from your country and your kindred and your father's house to the land that I will show you. ² And I will make of you a great nation, and I will bless you and make your name great, so that you will be a blessing. ³ I will bless those who bless you, and him who dishonors you I will curse, and in you all the families of the earth shall be blessed. ⁴ So Abram went." Genesis 12:1-4 (ESV)

God Will Meet You In The Go

That was a season of my life in which God used to fully transform me. Certainly there have been so many other seasons since then but it was something unique about that one. I found out for myself that if I tried God that I could fully trust God. Can I make the argument to you that God can still be trusted? During the passing of my mother some years later I found out that God could still be trusted. When my daughter transitioned one month after my mom, I found out that God could still be trusted. I've endured many ups and downs, trials and tribulations, pains and disappointments, but through them all it is yet my testimony that God can still be trusted. So as for me and my house it is still a go.

In 2013 famed Gospel artist and writer Tye Tribbett released a song entitled "Same God." Tribbett goes on to write in the lyrics, "If He did it before, He can do it again. Same God right now, same God back then." This bespeaks of God's faithfulness and His consistency.

Theologically, it is an expression of His immutability. Immutability is the doctrine that God does not change. With respect to God's promises and His love for us, He is immutable. If God promised to provide, His promises are still true. If God promised His presence, His promise is still true. If God has shown Himself trustworthy, guess what, He can still be trusted. His love for us is not circumstantial. Whatever He has been for you, He still is that yesterday, today and forevermore.

Notes

_____

_____

_____

_____

_____

_____

_____

_____

_____

Chapter Eight

Let's Go

~~*I'm tired*~~

~~*It's too cold*~~

~~*It's too hot*~~

~~*It's raining*~~

~~*It's too late*~~

Let's Go

Unknown

⁴ So Abram went, as the Lord had told him. Genesis 12: 4 (ESV)

At the age of seventy-five Abram left his country, his family and his father's house in route to an unknown destination. Yes, he was literally relocating to a new land but also spiritually, God was calling him from an old life with plans of a new life ahead. Many scholars and theologians regard this moment as one of the most significant moments in the history of the world. The building up of Israel as God's people began with this calling of Abram to go from familiarity to becoming the father of faith. Without hesitation or procrastination he went. Without a plethora of information and data to extensively study, he went. Without being able to fully articulate what he believed the plan to be, he went. Without have knowledge of what he may encounter along the way, he went. At seventy-five years old he wasn't as spry as he once was. I'm sure that he fatigued much quicker, I'm sure that he walked much slower, wasn't able to run as fast or even do quite as much. With all of that against him, he went. With a lack of clarity and much uncertainty, he went.

What an amazing display of faith and trust. Abram's story is a great example for us all of how we might achieve in spite of. It is a testament of what's ahead of us if we take a leap of faith. Peter would not have become a water walker had he not gotten out of the boat. Saul does not become Paul had he not gone to Straight Street. Had Moses not left the desert under God's direction, he does not become the historical biblical figure that we recognize him to be. The truth of the matter is that we will never find out what else we can be if we stayed in the same place. I would argue that the creative in you needs uncertainty. You will never fully discover you if you don't go.

Like Abram, every one of us has a story. Maybe your story is not one where age is a primary factor. Maybe it's not one where God has commanded you to leave your home. Maybe your story is one of poverty. Maybe it's a story of having to overcome a disability. Whether you are an ex-convict, ex-wife, an ex-husband or an ex whatever, it is your story. Abram teaches us that whatever your story may be, it's not too late to go. There is purpose on your life. God has predestined you to move beyond your circumstances. God has destined you to move beyond your realm of comfort and comprehension. The Apostle Paul teaches us in Romans 8: 28-30

28 And we know that for those who love God all things work together for good, for those who are called according to his purpose. 29 For those whom he foreknew he also predestined to be conformed to the image of his Son, in order that he might be the firstborn among many brothers. 30 And those whom he predestined he also called, and those whom he called he also justified, and those whom he justified he also glorified. 31 What then shall we say to these things? If God is for us, who can be against us?

Can I suggest to you that you are without excuse? Let's go.

January 2014 my wife and I made the choice to trust God. We did not have a denominational backing. We did not have a spiritual covering. We did not have financial support. Many of our friends and family members were obviously unsupportive. Those who appeared to be with us eventually fell by the wayside. However, we made a faith decision to trust God and go. To be completely honest, this new journey looked a lot like what I had experienced. I've always had to scratch and claw just to compete. I've never had the luxury of being a front-runner. I've been an underdog all of my life. In other words, God had prepared me for this.

God Will Meet You In The Go

I'll never forget that day. It was near freezing temperature; both rain and sleet began to descend upon the streets of Memphis. If anyone had plans to leave his or her home on that day it would have been justified to reconsider. Yet our resolve would not allow us to fold. God had called us out of the boat and we refused to get back in. Let's go was the unspoken declaration that we would share and impart into our team. At three o'clock on a cold, wet Sunday afternoon we launched the Redemption Life Church. In the cafeteria of our local community school there was over three hundred people, who in spite of the weather and everything else were in attendance. Pastors from all over the city were present, government officials were present, local media publications were there documenting the service. Never in a million years would I have expected such an amazing outpouring of support.

In over five years of ministry, Redemption has led hundreds of souls to Christ. Overwhelmingly over 90% of our water baptisms have been men of various ages. Our outreach initiatives have blessed thousands in our community. We currently have members in at least three states. I can't accurately quantify the true measure of our ministry statistically. However, the point that I'm making is that these things are not accomplished had we not decided to go. As I write to you I speak from experience when I say that God will meet you in the go. What are you waiting on? Let's go!

Nicholas James Vujicic is an Australian Christian evangelist and motivational speaker. That doesn't sound all that astounding, except Nick was born with tetra-amelia syndrome, which is a very rare disorder (called phocomelia). Nick was born without fully formed limbs or in his case there's the absence of both arms and legs. He experienced a life of difficulties, to say the least. He's survived bullying, depression and even an attempted suicide only to see God work wonders in his life. He has become a New York Times Best-Selling author with several worldwide publications. He's the Founder, President and CEO of Life Without Limbs, a non-profit organization that has made impacts all over the world. This man with no limbs has traveled to over fifty-seven countries and has shared his story with millions. Can I ask you a question? What is your excuse? With every advantage that you have, why aren't you moving? In this season you cannot allow limitations to limit you. You cannot allow obstacles to obstruct you. Let's go!

Let me pray for you. Father God in the name of Jesus I pray for every reader. I pray that each of them would sense a calling to go. Maybe their life is good already but I believe that you are calling them to greater. Maybe they're comfortable where they are but I pray now that you would crash their comfort zone. I pray that this book serves as a means of preparation and that You would give them clarity as to who and what to depart from. Cause them to move now God, even with their fears and uncertainties. As they go through the journey of life, I pray for supernatural provisions and that all of their needs will be met. I pray for divine protection as they tear down cultural norms and traditions. I pray for influence and inspiration. In your name I am believing that every reader would surrender now and give unto You a complete YES. This is my prayer in Jesus name. Amen.

Notes

_____

_____

_____

_____

_____

_____

_____

_____

_____

Acknowledgements

To my wonderful, beautiful and bad wife Samantha, thank you for being my better half. After Jesus you are the second best decision I have ever made. You push me to be better. You bring out the best in me. Thank you for sharing the ups and downs of life with me. I love you to life. Let's go.

To my children whom I love and live for, Devin Jr., Miyah, Kayla, Christion, and David. I'm so proud of each one of you. I'm blessed to have uber creative and gifted children who love God. Please know that everything I do is to set you all up to be better than I could ever be. I speak greatness over each one of you. Yet I give to you the gift of responsibility. Steward it well.

To my mother, the late Rev. Elaine R. Westbrook, thank you for parenting me, nurturing me, cultivating me, pouring into me, and pushing me into purpose. I'm standing on your shoulders. It is because you saw something in me that I believed in it as well. You spoke into my life and thus changed my life. I'm honored to be your son. I love you forever.

To my Redemption Church family, thank you for allowing me to completely be who God called me to be. You all have suffered through losses with me and have celebrated the wins with me as well. Thank you for unleashing me and supporting me. We're not just a church we are a family. Let's continue to change the game.

To Dr. Vernon, Lady Vernon and the entire Shepherds Connection family, thank you for sharing your visions, creativity, your minds and your strategies with me.

You all helped me to see that there is more. I'm truly grateful for the koinonia that I share with each of you. Change or die.

To Dr. James L. Netters and the Mt. Vernon Baptist Church family. I am forever grateful to have grown up in such an environment. Mt. Vernon has shaped so much of who I am. I was baptized there, received my calling there and had my first opportunity to practice ministry there. Dr. Netters you set such a standard of what a man of God is that even now I chase that standard. Thank you.

To Kelvin Bates, to be honest this project doesn't happen without you. When you said, "Go ahead and write this book," your words ignited something in me. Thank you for pushing that button. Thank you for opening doors for me both vocationally and professionally. I'm grateful for our relationship.

To everyone else whose names are too many to write, thank you for the inspiration, thank you for the love, the encouragement, the motivation and anything else that was either said or done which made a deposit into my spirit. I love you all. Let's go.